Business and Biodiversity

A Guide for the Private Sector

World Business Council for Sustainable Development — WBSCD
IUCN — The World Conservation Union

ISBN: 2-8317-0404-9

June 1997

Citation

Stone, D., Ringwood, K., Vorhies, F. 1997. Business and Biodiversity — A Guide for the Private Sector

This report was compiled for IUCN and WBCSD by:

David Stone

Conservation Advisory Services, Chemin des Clyettes, CH-1261 Le Muids, Switzerland

Kristina Ringwood

Project Manager, WMC Limited, Level 16 IBM Centre, 60 City Rd, Southbank, Victoria 3006, Australia;
currently on secondment to the
WBCSD, 160 Route de Florissant, CH-1231 Conches-Geneva, Switzerland

Frank Vorhies

Economist, Biodiversity Policy Coordination Division,
IUCN, Rue Mauverney 28, CH-1196 Gland, Switzerland

Acknowledgements

The authors would like to thank Glaxo Wellcome Plc for its role as champion of the WBCSD biodiversity project. In particular, we thank Mark Rhodes for his support, WMC Limited for the secondment of Kristina Ringwood to this project at the WBCSD, members of the WBCSD for case study information, and members from both organizations for their comments on the text.

A L'IV Communications Production

Table of contents

Executive summary

The world's biological resources are used every day by industry – the agricultural, pharmaceutical and forestry industries to mention but three. However, the Earth's resources are limited and concern has been growing about the way in which they have been managed.

Response to a common concern

The Convention on Biological Diversity is a major international response to managing the Earth's biological resources. Its objectives are:

- the **conservation** of biological diversity
- the **sustainable use** of its components
- the **equitable sharing** of its benefits

These objectives are extremely broad in scope and have the potential to affect all business sectors by:

- restricting long-term access to land and biological resources
- imposing more stringent environmental impact assessments
- introducing restrictions on the trade in biological products
- being of growing concern to investors and other stakeholders

The conservation and sustainable use of biological resources remains a major challenge to governments, conservation organizations, the private sector and members of the public. The future needs and objectives of all concerned parties come together on this common ground. Despite the Convention's potential impact on many business activities, business has not so far been closely involved in the Convention process. Conservation groups, on the other hand, have contributed actively. Unless business takes prompt steps to involve itself, it runs the risk of being excluded from the policy debates now under way – with severe and long-lasting implications for many sectors.

Taking your needs into account

This guide has been devised specifically to represent business interests, to tell business people how to become more engaged in implementing the Convention, and to encourage the private sector to contribute its valuable experience to the process under way. To achieve this, the guide proposes a medium-term work program for business. The information in this guide is both theoretical and practical and has been designed to be as relevant to the chief executive officer as it is to corporate or environmental affairs managers or local site managers.

At the same time, we hope it will also serve as an introduction for conservationists to the way business manages biodiversity. The report argues that the opportunities provided through the Convention will help businesses to work more closely with conservation organizations – to their mutual benefit. However, for such partnerships to develop successfully, business people must have a clear understanding of the implications of the Convention.

Partners for progress

The guide has been written by IUCN — The World Conservation Union in conjunction with the World Business Council for Sustainable Development (WBCSD). It is only through such unique partnerships that sustainable solutions can be found to address issues such as resource depletion and the long-term management of the Earth's biological resources.

About this guide and how to use it

This guide is a joint publication by the World Business Council for Sustainable Development (WBCSD) and IUCN — The World Conservation Union. In a close partnership, our two organizations are attempting to bring together valuable insights and experiences from two different perspectives which are increasingly converging on the same objective – that of ensuring that the world's wealth of natural resources is there for future generations.

It has been largely written by IUCN, the world's leading conservation body, which has developed the background and key components of the Convention on Biological Diversity. The WBCSD has contributed to the guide by providing business insights on the key issues of the Convention, developing a company management program for biodiversity and by supplying a series of case examples, primarily from member companies of the WBCSD. These case examples set a benchmark for environmental performance for other industries.

The guide's aim is to explain why business should be involved in the biodiversity debate and to suggest how it can participate. It explains the main principles of the Convention on Biological Diversity and describes some of the Convention's potential implications. It also examines the many linkages between biodiversity and the private sector and highlights the need for a new, more rational approach to the manner in which biological resources are used and managed.

Although the guide sets out to discuss a wide range of perspectives, there are certain limitations which need to be taken into account in a document of this size. For example, we have not been able to include an analysis of the financial implications of implementing the Convention.

The guide begins with an explanation of the importance of biological diversity. This is followed by an overview of the Convention on Biological Diversity and an examination of how decisions regarding the management of natural resources might influence the future of business worldwide. Section 5 examines some of the main issues and opportunities for involving the private sector in the Convention process. A range of case examples from a broad spectrum of the industrial world (mostly from WBCSD members) has been supplied to demonstrate the many ways in which business is already involved with caring for the Earth. These examples are presented in Section 6. Section 7 examines the potential for closer collaboration between the business and conservation sectors. The guide concludes with a glossary of biodiversity terms, a list of key organizations, and reference sources.

The implications of international agreements such as the Convention on Biological Diversity are often at first hard to grasp. We hope that, through the use of this guide, business people will be able to understand the process by which the language of the Convention is to be turned into action, and discover from it how and why they should now become involved. Its contents have been designed to inform and assist a wide range of people in the business world, including:

- the chief executive officer, who needs a summary of the main issues and of the Convention's effect on individual companies

- the corporate affairs manager, who needs to understand key biodiversity issues from the point of view of a conservation group and to learn how and where to participate to represent the company in key biodiversity meetings. It will also help the manager develop and implement policy for the company at the international, national and local levels

- the environmental manager, who will benefit from studying case examples of other companies' experiences in managing biodiversity and will implement the methodology which the guide proposes for managing biodiversity at the company level

- the site manager, who needs to understand how a local operation can implement the objectives of the Convention and thereby support the country's national biodiversity strategy. Financial costs and the benefits of biodiversity also need to be taken into account

But it is not only business people who we believe will benefit from the guide. By highlighting some of industry's concerns and drawing attention to the many ways in which different businesses already manage biodiversity, the guide aims to give conservation organizations a better understanding and appreciation of the needs and concerns of the private sector.

At the practical level, the guide provides many valuable examples of how business can constructively engage with the public sector in sustaining biodiversity. Among them are examples of collaboration between businesses from the developed world and governments from the developing world. In offering these examples, the guide provides a clear message that these parties share a common goal – a goal that can only be achieved through cooperation and the forging of partnerships.

Through this approach – combining the theoretical with the practical – we hope that the needs of all parties will be met by the guide. We hope, too, that through the experiences shared in this guide, each party in the debate will have a better understanding of the position of others. As a result, greater inspiration and closer working relationships will develop. The challenge for business is to get involved in conserving biodiversity sooner rather than later.

We are glad to have had the opportunity to collaborate on this important document.

David McDowell
IUCN Director General

Björn Stigson
WBCSD Executive Director

"Conserving the world's biological diversity is a matter of vital importance in itself. It is also essential that our natural resources are used in a sustainable way for the benefit of people throughout the world. The Convention on Biological Diversity sets the international framework for the conservation of biodiversity and business needs to be fully involved in its development and implementation. This guide presents very clearly how and why this should be done. As a primary supporter of this project, I am sure that it will play a key role in alerting the business world to the importance of the Convention."

Sir Richard Sykes
Chairman and Chief Executive, Glaxo Wellcome plc

1. Why should the private sector be concerned with biological diversity?

One of the major challenges facing the world community as it seeks to replace unsustainable development patterns with environmentally sound and sustainable development is the need to activate a sense of common purpose on behalf of all sectors of society. The chances of forging such a sense of purpose will depend on the willingness of all sectors to participate in genuine social partnership and dialogue, while recognizing the independent roles, responsibilities and special capacities of each.

Agenda 21: Earth's Action Plan, Chapter 27

Biological diversity affects us all. Life-sustaining systems such as clean air, productive oceans, fresh water and fertile soils depend upon a healthy and well-balanced environment. If this process is impaired or disrupted, life on Earth could not proceed as it does today.

The simplest measure of conservation is at the species level, where there is enormous variety and diversity. For example, about 250,000 plant species are known, while there may be as many as one million species each of fungi and bacteria. Many more species of plants and animals, particularly invertebrates, await discovery.

Beyond the level of species, there is a huge range of unique ecological systems, sustaining different populations and providing a basis for continuing diversity. Such diversity is of great importance for industries such as pharmaceuticals and agriculture as it provides them with a rich source of genetic materials. Some of those materials are likely to contain unique compounds or properties which, one day, may provide remedies for currently untreatable diseases.

We look in more detail in Section 2 at what biodiversity means. For the present, let us merely note that it is coming more and more under threat. Although precise figures cannot be given for the number of species being

The Convention on Biodiversity could affect almost every business sector. But it is not set in tablets of stone and the process of developing it continues. Business therefore needs to understand what the Convention is about and how to help shape the outcome.

lost each day, it is clear that the species extinction rate has accelerated in recent decades. Even if each loss seems trivial by itself, cumulatively it diminishes the capacity of the global environment to respond to change. It is not only the pharmaceutical industry which will suffer from these losses. As this guide will show, although few of us in the private sector view ourselves as being in the environment business, we are nonetheless all affected because the measures we take – or don't take – ensure that we have an impact on conservation and sustainable development in the long-term.

Convention on Biological Diversity

The Convention on Biological Diversity, launched in 1992 at the United Nations Conference on Environment and Development, was a crucial step towards securing biodiversity for the future. In Section 3 we examine the Convention in detail. It will suffice here to note that, given the range of views which had to be accommodated within the document, it is inevitably a broad statement of principles rather than a specific set of rules.

Nonetheless, the Convention is extremely comprehensive in scope and could potentially affect all sectors of business by:

* restricting long-term access to land and biological resources
* imposing more stringent environmental impact assessments
* introducing restrictions on the trade in biological products
* being of growing concern to investors and other stakeholders

Opportunities for business in the Convention

Because so many industries rely on using, or having access to, natural resources of one type or another, it is clearly in their best interest to ensure that the supply of those resources is not interrupted, diminished or lost forever. Despite this resource dependency and the Convention's potentially wide-ranging effect on the private sector, business has not so far actively involved itself in the development process.

Yet there are many windows of opportunity for private organizations to become involved in the continuing Convention process. Unless these opportunities are taken, companies and even whole sectors of the business community risk being excluded from the policy debates now under way. The implications of that exclusion could be severe and long-lasting. Management therefore needs to understand the current issues and to become involved.

In Box 1, we illustrate some of the ways in which business and the Convention intersect. It will be clear from this that business can no longer afford to sit on the sidelines.

Business activities can interact with the goals of conservation and sustainable use in a wide variety of ways. If your business is involved in any of the following, you will almost certainly be affected by decisions being taken under the Convention on Biological Diversity:

✓ Conducting operations in a biologically sensitive area
✓ Conducting operations in a conservation area and using land as a buffer zone
✓ Rehabilitating sites following intervention, for example reforestation following mining or forestry operations
✓ Supporting local biodiversity projects such as local parks or botanical gardens
✓ Securing contracts for access to biological resources in tropical forests, coral reefs or other ecosystems
✓ Using intellectual property rights for products developed from biological resources
✓ Supporting and/or training scientists in developing countries to conserve biodiversity or to screen biological materials
✓ Using traditional knowledge of biological resources
✓ Encouraging and developing effective partnerships between a company, local government authorities, non-governmental organizations (NGOs) and local communities in managing projects which interact with the environment
✓ Financing biodiversity projects, such as protecting endangered species or eco-efficient technology, that are managed by environmental NGOs, local communities, universities or other private groups
✓ Developing and using guidelines for biotechnology
✓ Undertaking biodiversity impact assessments

Box 1

Why business needs to focus on biological diversity

Responding to the challenge

Although business in general has not yet fully woken up to the implications of the Convention, a number of individual companies have already provided considerable support to the process, notably by taking the lead in adopting development, management and marketing strategies that favor biodiversity. In Section 6, we provide examples of industries which are already managing biodiversity effectively and creatively. However, for business as a whole to be more active in the Convention process, many more companies need to understand how it could affect their activities.

Business needs to realize that the Convention is not just about locking up large areas of land for conservation purposes. One of its main objectives is the sustainable use of the planet's biological resources and so involves the sustainable development of resources such as forests and fisheries. This objective is the key to much of industry's involvement in implementing the Convention. Another consideration for the private sector is the need to define and identify opportunities in the conservation and sharing of benefits accruing from resource development.

2. Understanding biodiversity

What is biodiversity?

The term "biodiversity" embraces the variety of all life on Earth. For many people, it is the natural resources they use – fuel wood, fruit, wild crops, fresh water, fish – or which they admire each day, the variety of species they observe and the way in which different species depend upon one another in respective ecosystems. At a more detailed level, biodiversity may be defined as the variability among living organisms and the ecological complexes of which they are part, including diversity within and between species and ecosystems. This is the definition which governments have adopted in the Convention on Biological Diversity.

The Earth's natural resources are under enormous pressure. The impact of a rapidly growing human population and the increasing demands for food, water and industrialization are the main causes for the loss of species and impoverishment of ecosystems. Deforestation, as a result of clear felling and slash-and-burn cultivation, together with soil erosion, pollution of inland and marine water bodies, and over-harvesting of species have all resulted in a serious depletion of the world's biodiversity.

> Conserving biodiversity is a lifeline for future generations, but population growth and society's demands for better living standards are putting it under increasing threat. **To conserve biodiversity, imaginative partnerships are needed, and these must include the business sector.**

Why is it important?

People have long realized the importance of biodiversity. Peruvian farmers, for example, have cultivated several hundred varieties of potatoes; several thousand varieties of rice have been identified in India. Conserving genetic diversity in this manner has been an important feature of many civilizations as it has helped them protect their crops from drought, diseases and pests. Yet few consumers are familiar with more than two or three of these varieties. Overall we have a poor understanding of the diversity and importance of these wild products.

Biodiversity is a vital component of the private sector, too. A wide range of biological resources is used in industry to provide foods, medicines, fabrics and an assortment of other products. Ensuring that these resources are continuously available is therefore essential for business.

Many enterprises have already taken measures that will help guarantee the long-term availability of their basic raw materials; others are now following suit.

Conserving biodiversity is a lifeline for future generations. Forests contain a vast range of resources, many of which have been developed into important food, medicinal and commercial products. They also help control and stabilize the Earth's climate and act as natural sponges, soaking up rainfall which helps prevent wide-scale run-off of water and soil. In a similar manner, rivers, lakes and oceans are a major source of fish and other species, many of which represent an important source of protein for rural communities in developing countries. Wetlands also play an essential part of the hydrological cycle as well as fulfilling other important ecological functions. Many of these processes are closely linked: the drainage of a wetland or diversion of a river course may cause irreversible consequences elsewhere.

In Box 2, we highlight some of the many benefits which the human race obtains from biological resources.

Box 2

The benefits of biodiversity

✓ Biological resources provide food, fuel, clothes, shelter and natural medicines
✓ Genes from wild plants and animals are frequently used to combat diseases and improve the production rates of many domesticated species. Without such genetic materials, many of our most important crops would have already succumbed, for example, to viral diseases
✓ Worldwide, medicines from wild products are worth some $40 billion each year
✓ Three plant species — wheat, rice and maize — provide half of the world's food. Add potatoes, barley, sweet potatoes and cassava and the total rises to three-quarters. Domesticated crops need to receive new protection from pests and disease every 5-15 years. Many of the new strains are derived from wild relatives of these plants
✓ Sustainable use and management of natural products can yield greater social and economic benefits than inappropriate harvesting. Fruit and latex from a single hectare of Amazonian forest can have a net economic value of $8400 per annum; harvested for wood pulp, this area of forest would provide a single return of about $3184

Where is it found?

Biodiversity is a global resource, but one with an uneven distribution. Countries with exceptional levels of biodiversity have been termed "megadiverse", and have been singled out by conservationists for priority attention. Examples include Brazil, Indonesia and Madagascar. These and several other countries contain phenomenal levels of endemic species – plants and animals which occur nowhere else on Earth. Brazil alone is thought to house one-third of the world's bird species, at least one-third of its plants and probably the same proportion of other species.

The majority of these ecological "hot spots" are in low- or middle-income countries where natural resources are often crucial to the livelihoods of millions of people. Protecting these resources is therefore not only about saving a particular species: emphasis has also to be given to maintaining the resources for the benefit of local communities and to assisting the country's economic and social development.

While tropical countries are home to the highest levels of biodiversity, many examples of important habitats lie outside the tropics. For example, many of the world's largest wetlands, and old growth forests in North America and Eurasia, provide fine examples of unmodified habitats. Fisheries resources are at their highest in and around some of the coldest waters on Earth. New evidence indicates that extremely high levels of biodiversity are found on the deep ocean floor.

Changing perceptions of biodiversity's importance

Human attitudes towards the use of biological resources are slowly changing. As people become aware of the links between the natural environment and many of their day-to-day activities, they are beginning to express their concerns in public, posing questions and demanding that governments act now to conserve these resources. In many countries, the environment has also become a strategic business opportunity. More and more companies are beginning to realize that, in association with industry and development, biological diversity can be a profitable investment.

Although it is difficult to place an economic price tag on the many products and services which derive from biological resources, it is clear that the functions they provide to the global economy could not easily be replaced – if indeed they could be replaced at all. Conservation of biodiversity therefore makes economic, as well as ecological, sense.

Working towards a common solution

It is not too late to act to prevent wide scale loss of biodiversity. However, conservation of biological resources will only be possible through broad cooperation and partnerships between the many constituencies interested and affected by biodiversity. Two key players are:

- the **private sector**, which is increasingly beginning to see the benefits from conservation and the sustainable use of biological resources (see Box 3)

- the **'biodiversity community'**, which to date consists mostly of government institutions and non-governmental organizations (NGOs), and which has now realized the need to collaborate with the private sector

For the Convention to be implemented in a way that promotes both ecological and economic processes, the Parties to the Convention need to work more closely with the private sector. This was clearly recognized at the 1996 meeting of the third Conference of the Parties to the Convention (COP), where several key decisions were made to work with the private sector in implementing the Convention. Those opportunities are examined in more detail in Sections 5 and 6.

Participating in the process

Greater transparency and participation is required on the part of all stakeholders. We believe that the private sector should seize the opportunities to work within the framework of the Convention and to become more closely involved with the decision-making processes. It should also accept a more responsible role in implementing and managing various

Box 3

Examples of
business initiatives
that conserve
biodiversity

Avenor Forestry Operations is helping conserve the biodiversity of more than 800 hectares of undisturbed old pines in Ontario, Canada. Management and research guidelines have been prepared to provide stakeholders with an improved understanding of how to manage forests with similar characteristics more effectively, and to carry out a detailed survey of the region's fauna and flora.

Glaxo Wellcome, in cooperation with **Pro-Natura International**, an NGO which specializes in tropical forest conservation programs, has developed a raft-like platform which rests on a forest canopy without damaging the trees. Currently being tested, this novel technique should permit scientists to get a more accurate picture of ecological processes in this micro-habitat. This unique facility should stimulate additional research from other chemical, agricultural and pharmaceutical companies. A proportion of the revenue obtained from the biological sampling will be contributed to the development of incentives for local conservation.

✓ Supermarkets and business chains are increasingly showing concern about environmental issues. Many companies now specialize in the manufacture and retailing of cosmetics, food, and pharmaceutical and hardware items which are derived from natural products. Most often this is in collaboration with local communities and business management units. Others, such as **Sainsburys** in the United Kingdom, have banned the use of certain fish oils because the harvesting of large numbers of these fish was having a serious effect on the dynamics of ocean food-chains.

✓ **NEC** is working with the **Wild Bird Society of Japan**, a local NGO, to follow the annual migrations of wild cranes between their breeding and wintering sites. The work has also included a wetland monitoring program in China, Japan, Korea, India, Mongolia and Russia. Based on the data obtained from these surveys, a request has been made to the respective governments to establish additional wetland protected areas.

conservation and sustainable-use programs. For their part, traditional non-governmental conservation groups should work more closely with the private sector than has hitherto been the custom. This is particularly vital in the search for ways of using resources in a sustainable manner that simultaneously provides long-term benefits to local communities.

The precise means of involving private sector partners in these programs will, of course, vary from one situation to the next. We give some examples of existing business initiatives in Box 3. As with the many other examples presented in Section 6, when a company adopts innovative approaches as part of its biodiversity policy, the result can be a greatly improved public image. What is more, it can provide a stimulus for investing wisely in the conservation and sustainable use of natural resources.

Such initiatives can perhaps be best addressed at the national level within the framework of national biodiversity strategies or national environment action programs (see also Section 4). This can be beneficial to all stakeholders. Indeed, by having already approved the strategies or programs, governments will clear the way for business to identify appropriate openings for collaboration.

Although considerable advances have been made in moving biodiversity to center stage, it is also clear that conserving biological diversity will remain a critical issue well into the 21st century. Groundwork for further action has already been identified by many countries. The Convention on Biological Diversity now serves to institutionalize and harmonize global efforts and to coordinate and implement the widest possible range of national actions.

3. The Convention on Biological Diversity

A response to global needs

Recent decades have witnessed growing concern over the continuing degradation and loss of biological diversity worldwide. This, coupled with a heightened awareness of development inequalities between countries or communities which have abundant biological resources and those wanting to conserve or harvest those same resources, led to the development of a multilateral agreement – the Convention on Biological Diversity (see Boxes 4 and 5).

The Convention is concerned with inequalities on sharing, having access to, and using, biological resources. Further, it recognizes that "economic and social development and poverty eradication are the first and overriding priorities of developing countries". Thus while biodiversity must be conserved, this conservation must take place in the context of sustainable development.

It is the strongest commitment to global conservation ever undertaken and thus serves as the best platform for linking development objectives with wise management of global biodiversity.

As a framework agreement, it lays the groundwork and guidelines for a wide range of issues which Contracting Parties and the broader sphere of those concerned with biodiversity need to address in order to conserve biodiversity while alleviating poverty.

Although the Convention may appear complex in structure, its objectives may be stated simply. They are:

- the **conservation** of biological diversity
- the **sustainable use** of its components
- the **fair and equitable** sharing of its benefits arising from this use

The Convention on Biological Diversity, signed by 150 nations at the Earth Summit in 1992, has three main aims: **conserving biodiversity, the sustainable use of its components, and the equitable sharing of its benefits.**

One of the main ways in which the Convention seeks to support private sector development is through the sustainable use of biological resources. Another is to identify new and additional financial resources and a third is to encourage existing financial institutions to invest in actions which will promote the conservation and sustainable use of biological resources.

Box 4

The making
of the Convention

Governments have long recognized the need for action to conserve biodiversity. This is reflected in the large number of national and regional treaties established to protect certain biological resources. It was not until the 1980s, however, that concern about the global environment led to the formulation of a number of international treaties.

The idea of a global convention for conserving biodiversity emerged from recommendations of the IUCN General Assembly in the mid 1980s. In 1987, the United Nations Environment Program (UNEP) established a working group on biodiversity. Although formal negotiations did not begin until November 1990, the Convention was concluded only 18 months later in May 1992. Issues covered in the final draft went far beyond original expectations. While the *in-situ* conservation of resources is a pivotal aspect of the Convention, many other far-reaching issues were also included. Among them were sustainable use, incentive measures, intellectual property rights, technology transfer, access to genetic resources, and financial mechanisms to assist countries to implement the Convention.

The Convention was signed by 150 countries at the United Nations Conference on Environment and Development in 1992 in Rio de Janeiro (the 'Earth Summit'), and entered into force in December 1993. By the end of 1996 it had been ratified by more than 160 countries and the European Union; notable exceptions include the USA. Contracting Parties are now working to implement the Convention.

Implementation begins once it has been ratified by governments. In ratifying it, governments recognize that they are responsible for conserving their national biodiversity and agree to take actions to ensure that the use of biological resources will be used in a sustainable manner.

National action plans

Another major action envisaged by the Convention is the development of national biodiversity strategies and action plans. The strategies include the systematic analysis of issues and options, as well as the establishment of agreements among public and private organizations on how to implement various provisions of the Convention. These will then be the basis of detailed programs setting out how the individual countries propose to manage their biological resources. These plans also help a company develop its biodiversity strategy. This is discussed further in Section 7.

The Convention sees collaboration, in the form of working partnerships between conservation organizations, businesses and governments, as an important step towards conserving national and global biodiversity.

Meeting the needs of many

The Convention is targeted at the broadest possible audience – from indigenous peoples and local communities, to national governments and international organizations. It is therefore intended to serve a wide range of interests – a goal which many recognize will be difficult to achieve.

The Convention has also gained credibility among member countries by placing responsibility for its implementation, and thereby for conserving the world's biological resources, with each individual nation.

As a global treaty, the Convention should also help strengthen the work of previously established conservation conventions, such as the Convention on International Trade in Endangered Species of Wild Fauna and Flora (CITES), the Ramsar Convention on Wetlands of International Importance, and the Bonn Convention on Migratory Species and their Habitats. In addition, it will influence the work of multilateral bodies such as the World Bank, the World Trade Organization (WTO) and the United Nations Environment Program (UNEP).

Box 5

The structure and
management of the
Convention

✓ The **Conference of the Parties (COP)** is responsible for taking decisions on implementing and monitoring the progress of the Convention. COP meetings are attended by government delegations from countries which have ratified the Convention. A wide range of observers may also attend: non-party countries, interested United Nations agencies and other international bodies, non-governmental organizations (NGOs), and the private sector. Three meetings have been held to date; the most recent (COP 3) was in Buenos Aires in 1996. COP 4 is scheduled for May 1998 in Bratislava.

✓ The COP advises Parties on measures taken to implement the provisions of the Convention and their effectiveness in meeting its objectives. It decides the work program for the Convention process.

✓ The Convention established a **Subsidiary Body on Scientific, Technical and Technological Advice (SBSTTA)** to assist with decision-making processes. Its main role is to provide scientific and technical advice to the COP on a broad range of issues related to biodiversity.

✓ The COP has decided that the **Global Environment Facility (GEF)** should oversee the funding mechanism on an interim basis. The GEF is a partnership between the World Bank, the United Nations Environment Program (UNEP) and the United Nations Development Program.

The **Secretariat for the Convention** is based in Montreal. Its contact details are:
Executive Secretary
Convention on Biological Diversity
393 St-Jacques Street, Room 300
Montreal, Quebec, Canada H2Y 1N9
Tel: +1 514 288 2220
Fax: +1 514 288 6588
E-mail: biodiv@mtl.net
URL: http://www.biodiv.org

4. Getting to grips with the Convention

As we have already noted, the Convention on Biological Diversity is the first global agreement to recognize that the conservation of biodiversity should be a common concern for everyone on Earth, and that it should become an integral part of the development process in each country.

It is a detailed framework which addresses biodiversity at various levels – genetic, species and ecosystems – within which national legislation strategies and action plans can be integrated. It represents a major step towards conserving biodiversity by placing responsibility for conservation at the national level with respective governments, and calls for governments to work together on a global agenda for biodiversity.

The components of the Convention

Comprising 42 articles, the text of the Convention is arranged in four main sections:

- Objectives, principles and jurisdiction (Preamble and articles 1-5)

- Commitments of each Party to conserve biological diversity and promote sustainable use of its components (articles 6-14)

- Relationships between the Parties on issues such as financial mechanisms, as well as the relationship between this Convention and other international treaties (articles 15-22)

- Administration and procedures through which the Convention will operate (articles 23-42)

A step-by-step guide to selected articles

So all-embracing is the Convention that there are few aspects that can be said to be of absolutely no relevance to business. However, in this Section we highlight those issues which we believe are of particular significance to the private sector. Box 6 lists the topics and the articles in which they appear.

These articles of the Convention are especially relevant to the development of partnerships between business and other parties concerned with conservation.

National biodiversity strategies	Article 6
Identification and monitoring	Article 7
In-situ conservation	Article 8
Ex-situ conservation	Article 9
Sustainable use	Article 10
Incentive measures	Article 11
Research and training needs	Article 12
Environmental impact assessment	Article 14
Access to genetic resources	Article 15
Technology transfer	Article 16
Technical and scientific cooperation	Article 18
Biosafety	Article 19
Financial resources	Article 20
Financial mechanism	Article 21

A need for strategic plans

Article 6 of the Convention requires Contracting Parties to develop national strategies which integrate conservation with sustainable development, for example by defining conservation areas or promoting the sustainable use of forests.

The broad coverage of environmental issues and concerns reflected in those strategies is intended to provide business and other interested groups with a solid platform from which to work towards sustainable development in collaboration with national authorities. A company's portfolio of interests should therefore take account of the national biodiversity strategies. We cover this aspect in Section 7.

Many national plans have already identified clear openings for businesses (see Box 7 for examples). Thus, guidelines for partnerships based on these earlier experiences, should be available. Indeed, some countries have already begun to invest in the development of national bodies to coordinate the actions of various businesses in line with the terms of the Convention. Nonethéless, there is still a great need for improved identification, monitoring and assessment of biological resources in many countries.

Many countries have developed an organizational infrastructure to oversee conservation and sustainable-use programs. The infrastructure may differ from one country to another but it often takes the approach shown in the following examples:

* **Costa Rica** and **Mexico** have both developed national biodiversity centers to facilitate inventory and monitoring activities — a vital first stage in cataloguing their natural resources and identifying genetic resources that could contribute to development programs, in general, and to human welfare, in particular.

* In **Indonesia** and the **Philippines,** National Environment Funds have been established to facilitate and encourage biodiversity investment and action by government, NGOs and the private sector.

Box 7

Capacity-building
for biodiversity

Sustainable use

Article 8, which deals with *in-situ* conservation, is the single most comprehensive article of the Convention. Essentially it aims to promote and maintain the diversity of species and ecosystems. Within such a broad remit, several aspects directly involve business.

Encouraging partners to assist with the conservation and management of protected areas is one goal for *in-situ* conservation – viewed as being the most efficient means of conserving a broad representation of biodiversity. One way in which this might be pursued is by supporting article 8(e), which seeks to "promote environmentally sound and sustainable development in areas adjacent to protected areas with a view to furthering protection of these areas". Or again, article 8(m) requires Parties to "Cooperate in providing financial and other support for *in-situ* conservation... particularly to developing countries".

Together with measures to promote *in-situ* conservation, the sustainable use of biological resources (article 10) lies at the core of the Convention. It is probably the most important article in view of the development objectives of business. It commits Parties to include conservation and the sustainable use of biological resources in their national decision-making processes, and it encourages them to develop and adopt measures which avoid or minimize harm to biodiversity. Under the article, Contracting Parties are also required to protect biological resources and to encourage their use in accordance with traditional practices compatible with conservation or sustainable-use.

One of the most powerful arguments used to encourage people to adopt and maintain this principle has been to demonstrate some of the social and economic benefits which can be obtained from the sustainable use of biodiversity.

Incentive measures

Developing incentive measures is a major part of the Convention. Article 11 states: "Each Contracting Party shall, as far as possible and appropriate, adopt economically and socially sound measures that act as incentives for the conservation and sustainable use of biological diversity." Many examples can be found which illustrate how, when local communities and other stakeholders are given responsibility for managing "their" natural resources, far greater efforts are made to maintain the balance between use and over-use. Later sections of this guide examine the importance of incentive measures to the private sector.

Applying local knowledge and practices

Involving the local community is one of the best ways of conserving bio-diversity, particularly when the community is brought into the decision-making process and into the management of natural resources. The Conference of the Parties (COP) has called on Parties to develop national legislation and strategies for implementing article 8(j) of the Convention. That article requires Parties to respect the knowledge, innovations and practices of indigenous and local communities and to encourage fair and equitable benefit-sharing with them. It also calls on them to supply information about what they are doing to implement that article and to submit case studies showing the measures they have taken to develop and implement the Convention in relation to indigenous and local communities.

A particular concern here has been the relationship between systems of indigenous knowledge and the intellectual property rights (IPRs) system. Concern has been expressed that patents may limit the rights of indigenous peoples to use traditional crop varieties and to receive appropriate returns from the application of traditional knowledge in the developed world.

Much debate still surrounds the issue of IPRs but the Convention has succeeded in bringing it closer than ever before to the center of the debate on conservation and sustainable use. Article 15 takes an important first step towards ensuring that benefits are more evenly shared because it recognizes the principle of national sovereignty over genetic resources and the resulting authority to regulate and control access to those resources.

In this respect, benefit sharing is encouraged not only between countries but also between users and local and indigenous communities. Article 8(j) referred to above and a number of other recommendations contained in articles 10(c) and 18.4, for example, are also intended to support the creation of incentives for local communities and to encourage their participation in benefit sharing.

Biosafety

One issue related to the use and prospecting of living biological resources (bioprospecting) which has raised concern has been the use of genetic materials. This is a topic which is still under debate in the Convention process.

The transfer and manipulation of genetic materials from plants and animals, through biochemical means, has brought many advances to medicine, agriculture and industry. At the same time, people are concerned about the potential risks to biodiversity and human health which are posed by living modified organisms (LMOs) – the term used in the Convention to define organisms which have been modified through biotechnology. Work has already begun on a protocol to the Convention which deals primarily, but not exclusively, with the safe use of LMOs.

Some countries already possess legislation designed to ensure the safe use of LMOs, but there are as yet no international agreements. The greatest concern revolves around the absence of rigid field testing of LMOs, as the interaction of these organisms with other natural species is unknown. For example, one area of concern is the possible threat to global biodiversity from this interaction leading to changes in 'non-target' species, by unbalancing long-established food webs and because the stability of the inserted genes is not always known.

Work is therefore under way, both at the national and international level, to develop biosafety guidelines to ensure that correct field testing and handling of LMOs takes place.

Financing biodiversity

A commitment to conserving biological diversity is dependent on there being adequate funds to implement and support actions. Article 20 states that each Contracting Party is requested to provide financial assistance and incentives to support national plans and priorities. The Convention recognizes, however, that economic and social development, as well as the need to overcome poverty, are priorities for many Parties from the developing world. Implementing the Convention in those cases could therefore depend on the commitment of Parties from the developed world.

To assist developing countries, article 21 provides for a financial mechanism to help them meet their scientific, economic and institutional obligations under the Convention. The Global Environment Facility (GEF) currently oversees the funding mechanism of the Convention.

Other funding institutions are also urged to ensure that their activities are more supportive of the Convention. The Executive Secretary of the Convention has also agreed to explore means of collaborating with other funding institutions and of involving the private sector in the work of the Convention. We return to this aspect in Section 5.

Information sharing

In addition to these specific issues, a number of common provisions of the Convention should also be considered by the business community. It mentions repeatedly the need for greater cooperation between nation states and organizations, particularly in the domain of public education and awareness (article 13), and the need to exchange information (article 17) and promote technical and scientific cooperation (article 18).

Cooperation and information-sharing is also central to articles 15 and 16, which respectively govern access rights to genetic resources and the transfer of technology, as well as to the handling of biotechnology and the distribution of its benefits (article 19). Much of the attention now being given to information sharing focuses on developing a Clearing-House Mechanism (CHM) for the use of Parties and other stakeholders, including the private sector. More details on this are given in the following section.

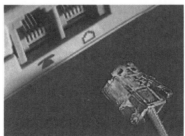

5. Issues and opportunities for the private sector in the Convention

The Convention offers many opportunities for business to participate in the process. **What are the issues, which sectors are affected and how should business respond?**

The private sector has an important contribution to make in conserving biological diversity and promoting sustainable development. Today, business is increasingly working towards the protection of the environment and is thereby contributing to a better standard of living for future generations. However, although many businesses have made considerable efforts to address these concerns, the majority have not yet begun to participate fully.

This section examines some of the key effects the Convention may have on a broad range of businesses. We also review some of the main business issues which need to be borne in mind in light of the current deliberations and forthcoming meetings of the Subsidiary Body on Scientific, Technical and Technological Advice (SBSTTA) and COP 4.

Issues for business

As we have already remarked, a poor understanding of the Convention on the part of business may be responsible for the low level of private-sector participation in the discussions which have taken place so far. Certainly, too many in the business world have failed to seize the opportunities and initiatives that would contribute to conserving biodiversity and global development.

This makes it doubly important that those concerned recognize how the Convention has the potential to affect the way business currently manages biological resources. Here are just some areas where the Convention's effects are likely to be felt:

✓ long-term access to, and availability of, biological resources
✓ restrictions on land and marine access for exploration and development
✓ more stringent requirements for environmental impact assessments

✓ national strategies to conserve biological resources
✓ restrictions on trade in products determined to be "biodiversity unfriendly"
✓ voluntary versus legislative measures to protect biodiversity
✓ liability for not protecting biodiversity
✓ strict codes for ensuring safety in biotechnology
✓ public perception in the marketing of "biodiversity friendly" products

Plainly, a company's involvement with conservation and development activities will vary from one situation to another. What is important, though, is that each enterprise develops a dialogue with other interested organizations, including conservation groups, and that it tries to identify an appropriate link with the Convention process.

We can only repeat that if business fails to involve itself in the rapidly developing Convention process it runs the risk of being excluded. What is more, if it fails to put forward its point of view, it forfeits any right to complain that its voice has been ignored.

The level of participation at COP meetings by conservation organizations and by business has been strongly skewed in favor of the former. For example, of the 1,000 participants at COP 2, about 140 were non-governmental organizations (NGOs) whereas only 20 were from business. Nevertheless, while the number of industries participating may still be quite small, it is encouraging to see that it is increasing and that more sectors are gradually becoming involved in the process. In particular, the pharmaceutical and seed-producing sectors, have expressed considerable interest in the development and workings of the Convention and have begun to participate by developing position papers on various articles under discussion and attending meetings at the national and international levels.

Which business sectors are most affected?

In order to emphasize the extent of the overlap between the issues which the Convention is concerned with and those which are of significance to business, we have devised Table 1, listing the Convention's main components horizontally against a selection of industries, displayed vertically.

Industry sectors	Convention components							
	National strategy	Incentive measures	Technology transfer	Intellectual property rights	Impact assessement	Biosafety	Equitable sharing	Indigenous people
Pharmaceutical	✓	✓	✓	✓	✓	✓	✓	✓
Biotechnology	✓	✓	✓	✓	✓	✓	✓	✓
Agriculture	✓	✓	✓	✓	✓	✓	✓	✓
Petroleum	✓	✓	✓		✓		✓	✓
Mining	✓	✓	✓		✓		✓	✓
Fisheries	✓	✓	✓	✓	✓	✓	✓	✓
Retail	✓			✓		✓		
Tourism				✓			✓	✓
Banking	✓	✓			✓		✓	✓
Energy	✓	✓	✓		✓			✓
Manufacturing	✓			✓	✓	✓	✓	✓
Forestry	✓	✓	✓		✓		✓	✓

The table shows clearly that biodiversity has a broad impact and that it is an essential foundation for development in many sectors. However, the table is not comprehensive because each business operation has specific circumstances and local issues to address. So, while the ultimate goal should remain the same, different enterprises may well have different priorities.

In Table 2, we show in more detail how the Convention impinges on a range of industries and highlight what the priorities of those industries are. It should be noted that several general considerations – for example, research, the training of local people, funding, and the conservation of land around operations – are common to all the sectors and so are not reported individually.

Pharmaceutical — A key issue for the pharmaceutical sector is to develop agreements for Intellectual Property Rights (IPRs) which simultaneously satisfy developing country concerns with respect to the equitable sharing of benefits while also meeting the industry's patent concerns. Other issues include the transfer of pharmacological expertise in bioprospecting; the transfer of results from research and development to local communities and indigenous peoples to address issues of equity sharing; and the development of international and national biosafety guidelines, notably through the negotiation of a protocol to the Convention.

Agricultural/Seed	Biosafety guidelines are being developed at international and national levels to control the safety of the trade in genetically modified organisms (GMOs).
Petroleum	Issues include: future restrictions on access to land, marine and coastal areas; the possible limitation of transport routes as a result of more detailed environmental impact assessments (EIAs); more stringent requirements for ecosystem monitoring; and greater participation by local communities and indigenous peoples in development projects, particularly with respect to technology-transfer and equitable-sharing issues.
Mining	There is the issue of future restrictions on access to land because of more detailed EIAs. Other issues include: the need for companies to develop biodiversity policies in accordance with national strategies; developing greater participation in mining projects with local communities and indigenous peoples in order to address issues of equity sharing. Biosafety could also become an issue as a result of the use of biological metallurgical processes to remove gold and other minerals from ore.
Fisheries	The institutional framework of the fisheries industry, including common access and subsidized fleets, is now being seriously questioned.
Retail	Retailers will increasingly request confirmation from producers that their products have been produced in a "biodiversity-friendly" manner.
Banking	The banking sectors will increasingly be looking to fund new "biodiversity-friendly" projects.
Energy	To take but one example: the hydro-electricity industry should be particularly concerned with preserving biodiversity and reducing the impact of its operations on the biodiversity of the large areas of land and water it manages.
Manufacturing	The main issues will vary depending on the location and the product and process of manufacture. For example, in developing countries, technology transfer will be an important consideration.

Forestry	The principal issue in the forestry sector is to ensure sustainable forestry management, including the conservation of biodiversity, through the use of adaptive forestry practices. Other issues include requirements for more detailed environmental impact assessments (EIAs) and ecosystem monitoring; consideration of national strategies; and participation in forestry projects with local communities and indigenous people.

Key issues and opportunities for business at COP 4

The importance of the interface between business and biodiversity was highlighted at COP 3 in 1996. A number of decisions which provide clear entry points for the private sector to involve itself in the lead up to COP 4 in 1998 were made (see the Calendar of Events in Section 7). Some of the entry points are at the global level and take the form of international meetings and deliberations on biodiversity. Others are at the country level and concern the national obligations set out by the COP decisions.

Business therefore has a range of opportunities through which to engage in both the global deliberations and the national implementation. These entry points are discussed below, and we return to them in Section 7. Essentially, they constitute a medium-term work program for engaging the private sector in the Convention process.

Natural resource sectors

The Parties to the Convention envisage biodiversity objectives being integrated into relevant sectoral policies in industries such as agriculture, forestry, fishing and mining. As the COP discussions unfold, there is a clear need for businesses engaged in harvesting and managing natural resources to participate, both to represent their sector's interest and to share their experiences with others.

Agriculture

Agricultural biodiversity was given special attention at COP 3. In particular, the Parties were interested in:

✓ the use of genetic resources for agriculture
✓ how benefits from using genetic resources were to be shared in the economy
✓ the inappropriate use of agrochemicals that affect biodiversity
✓ managing the risks associated with the use of living modified organisms from biotechnology

Accordingly, the Parties have decided to establish a program on agricultural biodiversity to "promote the positive effects and mitigate the negative impacts of agricultural practices on biological diversity"; it will also promote the objectives of the Convention with respect to "genetic resources of actual or potential value for food and agriculture". The program will identify and assess relevant current activities and will aim to achieve a sharing of experiences and the transfer of knowledge and technologies.

Where appropriate, the program will be carried out in conjunction with the United Nations Food and Agriculture Organization (FAO), taking into account any recommendations from SBSTTA 3.

Marine

Marine biodiversity was actually covered in November 1995 at COP 2 in Indonesia, from which the "Jakarta Mandate" was produced. This document outlined a program directed at the conservation and management of marine and coastal biodiversity. Among the issues included were: integrated marine and coastal ecosystem management; the sustainable use of marine resources; sustainable 'mariculture' practices; and the management of, and restrictions on, the introduction of alien species. All of these have a significant bearing on private fisheries and other institutions which use marine and coastal resources.

Forests

The Parties noted that the Convention's objectives "must be an integral part of sustainable forest management practices". In this respect, the COP Secretariat has been requested to develop a work program on forest biodiversity which should begin by focusing on the design of technologies and management systems necessary for maintaining forest biodiversity.

In addition, SBSTTA has been directed to consider "scientific analysis of the ways in which human activities, in particular forest management practices, influence biological diversity and assess ways to minimize or mitigate negative influences".

Other sectors and issues

In-situ conservation

The serious interest of the Parties in *in-situ* conservation provides several opportunities for private sector involvement. One particular area which is expected to become of greater interest is habitat restoration. Here, the Parties will be looking towards business not only with a view to securing a stronger commitment to habitat restoration but also to benefiting from its knowledge and experience.

Another related conservation topic which has attracted the attention of the Parties is the role of indigenous and local communities in maintaining *in-situ* biodiversity. The Convention Secretariat plans to hold a workshop at which governments, indigenous and local communities, and other relevant bodies will examine how traditional knowledge about biodiversity interacts with other forms of knowledge, and will discuss the influence of current laws and policies on traditional knowledge and what part incentive measures can and should play.

Genetic resources and technology

The COP continues to pay considerable attention to the issues of access to genetic resources and the transfer of technology. At COP 3, governments were asked to collect information on their policy measures and guidelines for access, as well as on their national participatory processes and research programs. Mindful of the fact that much of this information would have to be specially gathered, the COP invited and encouraged governments to generate it in collaboration with relevant stakeholders. We believe that businesses in sectors such as biotechnology should ensure that their expertise is represented in this process so that the resulting guidelines properly reflect the interests of all stakeholders.

Intellectual property rights (IPRs)

The COP recognizes that there may be difficulties with the implementation of IPRs. The COP Secretariat is working to provide relevant information on IPRs to evaluate the situation in more detail. The COP is especially interested in cooperation with the World Trade Organization (WTO) and the World Intellectual Property Organization on Trade-Related Aspects of Intellectual Property Rights (TRIPS). This is an area which may also have serious implications for the private sector. It therefore makes good business sense for the Secretariat to be furnished with relevant information from private sector perspectives.

Financial resources

The funding of activities which promote the conservation and sustainable use of biological resources is an issue of central concern to the Convention. The COP is therefore searching for ways to increase the flow of funds to biodiversity projects, especially from developed to developing countries. Specific areas which the private sector should be aware of include:

✓ **The Global Environment Facility (GEF)**
   The GEF provides finance to developing countries as well as to countries with economies in transition, in support of the Convention's objectives and actions. GEF funding is usually directed to government organizations and occasionally to non-governmental organizations (NGOs), but it is also experimenting with financing private sector activities through the International Finance Corporation (IFC), the private sector division of the World Bank Group. GEF funds channeled through the IFC have often served to leverage additional private sector finance. The COP Secretariat will provide COP 4 with a review of the GEF, including an assessment of its ability to secure that additional private finance.

✓ **Additional financial resources**
   In their decision on additional financial resources, the Parties called on "all funding institutions... to strive to make their activities more supportive of the Convention". They also invited those institutions to provide the Secretariat with information on how

their activities were supporting the Convention. Traditionally, the focus has been on funding from government bodies and NGOs, but the Parties now want to "explore further possibilities for encouraging the involvement of the private sector in supporting the Convention's objectives". The Secretariat was asked to carry out such a study, and this too will be presented at COP 4.

As most of the capital now flowing from developed to developing countries is private, there is a growing interest in exploring options for ensuring that these flows are good for biodiversity. Building on private sector support for initiatives such as those of the United Nations Environment Program (UNEP) on banking and environment, and insurance and environment, we believe there is now an exciting new opportunity to focus on private financing of biodiversity conservation.

Incentive measures

Incentive measures were directly addressed at COP 3 for the first time since the Convention came into force. The issue appears throughout the COP's decisions on matters such as agricultural biodiversity, forest biodiversity and *in-situ* conservation.

The COP has now called on Parties to review existing legislation and economic policies in order to identify enabling incentive measures and to take appropriate action on those incentives that threaten biological diversity. The need for case studies which allow the Parties to share experiences has also been recognized.

Parties have been encouraged to set up capacity-building and training programs and to promote private-sector initiatives in this regard. The COP clearly sees a role for the private sector in building national capacities to design, implement and monitor incentive measures for biodiversity. These issues are likely to be addressed in more detail at SBSTTA 3 and COP 4.

Clearing-House Mechanism (CHM)

Sharing information and experiences will be crucial to the successful implementation of the Convention, both at the national and the local level. A CHM is being developed to provide such a facility.

Parties now realize the great opportunities which the Internet has to offer and have called on the Secretariat to set up a CHM homepage (http://www.biodiv.com). Some Parties have already begun to link their national CHM homepages to that of the Secretariat.

Though access to the Internet is spreading rapidly, there remains a need for capacity-building and training on information systems technology, especially in developing countries. Business has the capacity to provide those resources, either on a commercial or a 'public service' footing, and also to assist in linking the world's institutions and expertise that are working to conserve biodiversity. In this connection, the COP instructed the Global Environment Facility (GEF) to provide funds in support of CHM initiatives in developing countries. This funding could possibly be used to leverage private-sector involvement.

The Parties have in fact emphasized that one of the key characteristics of the CHM is that it "should to the extent possible involve the private sector". The sharing of information relevant to biodiversity must include information relevant to decision-making in the private sector as well as in the public sector. To this end, the Secretariat has been requested "to identify those activities and organizations which could support the CHM and to provide appropriate advice to the SBSTTA at its next meeting". This provides business with a real opportunity to inform the Parties how they can support the development of the CHM.

Emerging issues

In addition to this wide range of continuing activities, two new focus areas are scheduled to emerge from the forthcoming SBSTTA 3 and COP 4 meetings:

- **An ecosystem focus on inland water systems.** This follows from earlier attention given to marine and forest systems. The private sector is very dependent on inland water, both for its production processes and as a means of transport, so this issue is potentially very important for industry to monitor and provide input.

- **Biodiversity impact assessment.** The Convention calls for biodiversity considerations to be integrated into environmental impact assessment procedures and for those procedures to be applied to relevant policies, programs and projects. In the context of the Convention, this means incorporating the objectives of conservation, sustainable use and benefit sharing into new procedures for biodiversity impact assessment. SBSTTA 3 will begin to consider this issue, which will again be taken up at COP 4. Business has considerable experience of carrying out environmental impact assessments and it could therefore make an extremely valuable contribution to the development of effective procedures for biodiversity impact assessments. We believe it should take this opportunity to contribute.

Windows of opportunity

We hope that this brief overview of some of the main recommendations arising from COP 3 shows that business now has an excellent opportunity to become more closely involved in the continuing dialogue on biodiversity and also to participate more actively in the Convention process. That engagement by business will, we believe, be warmly welcomed by the COP, which has on many different occasions invited private sector involvement. In its decision on incentive measures, for example, the COP notes that "the private sector has an important role in the design and implementation of incentive measures".

So the opportunity is there to make a contribution. It is now up to business to seize it.

6. Sharing experiences: case examples on business and biodiversity

Although many sectors of industry still have much ground to make up on biodiversity, **we cite here some notable examples of companies and business organizations that have made progress by taking the initiative.**

Many business sectors are already managing biodiversity as part of their normal day-to-day operations. Some of those initiatives are specific actions within a given sector – for example, reducing the impact of an exploratory drilling site or developing a management plan for a particular forest. Others follow a much broader approach and can be applied to a wide range of applications.

A closer look at some of the initiatives which have been developed between business and conservation organizations should help both groups to better focus on identifying potential areas of collaboration.

Forestry and biodiversity

The forestry sector has long been a sensitive interface between conservation organizations and industry. But it is not only the conservation aspects of forestry about which concern has been aired: social, economic and ecological considerations have also often been at the heart of such discussions.

Some conservation organizations want to see an outright ban on logging but a growing number now prefer to view forests as valuable assets of host countries. Proposed consumer boycotts on timber exports can produce undesirable outcomes on national and local economies. They may also have undesirable social and environmental effects. The abrupt loss of export markets, for example, can lead to forests being converted to other uses or their production being diverted to a less efficient domestic market. Developing incentive measures for the sustainable use of forests has therefore featured high on the agenda in recent years.

The result has been a suite of innovative and practical solutions, many of which are in keeping with the principles of the Convention on Biological Diversity. Although systems such as eco-labelling are intended to ensure that countries produce more sustainable products, it is important to recognize that the measures can be distorted into technical barriers to trade. Where eco-labelling is applied, producers and retailers are required to provide information on the source of the materials – the final decision about whether to buy the products rests with the consumer. Within the forestry sector, forest certification is one innovative tool which is already having a positive impact by providing a market incentive for improved forest management, for example, through the voluntary Forest Stewardship Council, the American Forest and Paper Association and other programs.

Finding local solutions to forest issues

Deforestation is a factor contributing to the loss of biodiversity. Many organizations are actively working to slow the rate of deforestation and to tackle the root causes of the problem. Some, such as the **Business Council for Sustainable Development for the Gulf of Mexico**, along with more than 20 collaborating groups from government, business, academic and public interests, are examining the benefits of farmland restoration in certain marginal soils in the Mississippi Delta. The aim is to determine whether hardwood reforestation could be competitive with soybean production.

Many members of the private sector are today engaged in similar management programs. In Alberta, Canada, a rehabilitation and revegetation project started by the **TransAlta Corporation** in 1968 has contributed greatly to increasing biodiversity. The sites, which now spread over more than 200 hectares, have been certified by the provincial government as having been satisfactorily reclaimed for wildlife habitat.

On a wider scale, the **Business Council for Sustainable Development for Indonesia** (including **Majelis Usahawan Indonesia**) has been influential in establishing natural, undisturbed forest plots within larger forestry concessions. In the long-term, the plots should play an important role in maintaining local biodiversity by acting as 'reservoirs' for plants and animals throughout the country.

In Canada, the "Unique Areas Program" operated by the **Bowater Mersey Paper Company** has established guidelines for conserving

natural areas whose unique botanical, zoological, geological, hydrological, cultural or scenic characteristics merit special attention. Sites for inclusion in the program may be proposed by the general public, government agencies or a company employee. Protection has already been afforded to a 156-hectare virgin stand of red spruce, hemlock and yellow birch, an old-growth stand of hemlock thought to be about 350 years old, and a permanent sampling plot which has been established to monitor ecological changes over time. The company intends to designate additional sites in future years so that a range of representative old-growth stands are set aside for conservation purposes.

Addressing CO_2 concerns

While many uncertainties surround current predictions about global warming, the topic is clearly one of major environmental and social concern. Accordingly, a number of businesses are already getting to grips with this issue. The **Dutch Electricity Generating Board**, for example, signed a Memorandum of Association with the **Face Foundation** in 1990 to establish 150,000 hectares of new forest within 25 years. As a result, reforestation is now under way in the Netherlands, Africa, Asia, Latin America and Central Europe. The thinking behind this scheme is that green plants absorb CO_2 from the air and store it as carbon for considerable periods of time. By supporting this reforestation program, the Dutch Electricity Generating Board expects that as many as 75 million tonnes of CO_2 might be sequestered from the atmosphere, so creating a buffer until it is possible to generate electricity in the Netherlands with a minimal emission of CO_2.

This approach works towards reducing the potential risks posed by higher concentrations of greenhouse gases in the atmosphere and it fits within the conditions of the Convention on Biological Diversity. The company has developed criteria for selecting projects based on the durable sequestration of CO_2. They include:

✓ the use of native species in establishing new forests
✓ avoidance of chemicals
✓ developing the interest of the forest owners in maintaining the forests
✓ the participation of local and regional populations

In Japan, the Tokyo Electricity Power Company uses microalgae for research into greenhouse gas sequestration because of their exceptionally high photosynthetic rate. The organisms also have the benefit of taking up much less space than other plants or crops sown for similar purposes. The resulting microalgae can also be used in a wide range of products, for example, in fertilizers, paper, fuel and medicines.

Pharmaceuticals and biodiversity

Biodiversity prospecting, or bioprospecting, for genetic resources is another resource-use that has captured considerable public and corporate attention in recent years. In particular, the value of biological diversity as a source of pharmaceutically active substances has been the subject of many studies. In Box 8 we cite some figures which show just what a rich source of medical products nature is.

Plants and animals are therefore of considerable importance for the development of medical products, both now and in the future, and this is one of the many reasons for conserving natural habitats, notably tropical forests which contain more species than any other single habitat. While nature's rich storehouse holds great promise for the pharmaceutical industry – and the number of companies which have already invested in bioprospecting shows that they understand its potential – the importance of many of these plants for local communities should not be overlooked.

Few regulations have hitherto governed bioprospecting. However, many aspects of the Convention on Biological Diversity will influence the manner in which plant and animal materials are obtained and used in future. Some of the most important concerns for business are:

✓ access to biological resources
✓ intellectual property rights
✓ technology transfer
✓ sharing of benefits
✓ the training of local counterparts and the development of research and management facilities

Box 8

The importance of
wild species

✓ At least 35,000 species of plants are estimated to be of medicinal value: to date, just 5000 have been studied in detail for medicinal applications.

✓ Surveys in the United States show that 118 of the top 150 prescription drugs were originally derived from living organisms: 74 per cent from plants, 18 per cent from fungi, 5 per cent from bacteria and 3 per cent from vertebrates.

✓ 50% of the top ten prescriptive drugs are based on natural plant products.

✓ China alone produces more than 40,000 different kinds of traditional plant drugs.

✓ The World Health Organization (WHO) estimates that 80 per cent of the people in developing countries rely on traditional plant-derived medicines.

Many businesses have already taken steps towards ensuring a more equitable system of sharing financial profits with national governments and even local communities. One of the first such initiatives was an agreement between scientists in Costa Rica and the US pharmaceutical group Merck and Company, which has funded a new joint exploration and development institution, INBio. Although earlier deals such as this have generated considerable controversy, they have served to stimulate dialogue between different groups and interests in exploring other potential means of collaboration. One of the most obvious immediate benefits of recent agreements is that they are far more transparent and the benefits which accrue to local partners are better attuned to their immediate and long-term needs.

Bioprospecting, if properly structured, remains a considerable hope for future conservation and development efforts. As more and more businesses become involved with new investigations, particularly in the cosmetic, food and pharmacological sectors, technological developments are being further refined and better use is being made of results. Attention is also slowly spreading from plants to other taxonomic groups, with particular interest being shown in bacteria, fungi, marine invertebrates and insects, all major groups which have been poorly examined to date.

The **Centre for Natural Product Research** in Singapore, in collaboration with the **National Science and Technology Board** and **Glaxo Wellcome**, is sourcing biological materials from the Asia-Pacific region. In addition to screening bio-active molecules from plants, fungi and bacteria for possible medicinal applications, the project has also played an important role in conserving biodiversity by training local scientists, creating employment and focusing greater attention on the value of selected natural products.

Mining and biodiversity

Exploration and prospecting for natural resources are vital activities for many businesses. In many areas, particularly in biologically sensitive environments, environmental impact assessments are increasingly required before exploration and development can begin. This is also noted in the Convention on Biological Diversity (article 14). Traditionally these assessments, together with the later exploitation or extraction of natural resources, have been a delicate area where business and conservation interests have often failed to see eye to eye.

The mining industry is aware of this concern and, in recent years, has made considerable efforts to ensure that its operations have as small an impact as possible on the local environment. Many companies have gone as far as to enrich the environment through careful rehabilitation programs once their operations have been completed.

Flora and fauna surveys were some of the first activities undertaken by **WMC Limited** when conducting exploratory drilling for gold in an ecologically sensitive region in Victoria, Australia. Areas where biologically important plants were found were excluded from the exploration program. The company laid particular emphasis on avoiding soil compaction and contamination, and on minimizing disturbance to the vegetation. Preventing the spread of invasive weeds was another concern. Through agreements with local communities and government, a program of soil sampling, geophysical testing and diamond drilling was successfully carried out with minimal impact on biodiversity.

Careful planning and wise management can clearly help minimize the adverse effects of mining or drilling operations. In cases where greater physical disruption is required in order to reach certain metals or minerals, site rehabilitation should become a priority. This can take many forms. Coastal dune sand mining in South Africa, for example, had caused a temporary change in the local environment. But, by removing the vegetation and topsoil ahead of the mining operation, **Rio Tinto's** planners in South Africa were able to replace them over the mined sand, effectively speeding up the rate of settlement and recolonization of the various ecological processes. Before the mining began, 243 plant species had been identified in the region: after 12 years, this diversity of species had returned, demonstrating a restoration of biodiversity. This type of restoration indicates the possibilities which mining industries can now use to counter claims that their activities are incompatible with environmental protection.

Inventories and monitoring

Habitat and species inventories are essential prerequisites for *in-situ* conservation. They can take many forms. In Turkey, for example, **Glaxo Wellcome** is funding a plant identification program with the aim of conserving important ecological sites and contributing to the overall knowledge of the country's botanical database. In collaboration with **Fauna and Flora International, Dogal Hayati Koruma Dernegi** – a local environmental NGO – and the Department of Pharmaceutical Botany, **University of Istanbul,** the geographical distribution of certain plant groups is being mapped in order to identify nationally important plant areas, which will allow vulnerable or endangered habitats to be identified. Fifty-three such sites have so far been identified and 30 species and subspecies have been confirmed as new to Turkey's flora. As a result of this classification, a program is being developed to ensure that priority habitats are protected and properly managed – a significant contribution to preserving the rich, but threatened, flora of the country.

Around its gold and nickel mining operations in Western Australia, **WMC Limited** has developed a land management system which classifies land at various levels into biophysical resource units, based on factors such as topography, landform, geomorphology, soil type, geology and vegetation structure. Ecological parameters, such as species richness, diversity and abundance can be sampled within the most homogenous unit. This allows information to be directly applied to management practices at local, regional or even national levels through the identification of ecological sensitivity and conservation values. This system is cost- and time-efficient and can be integrated into the planning, development, operating and closure phases of mining operations.

In Canada, a study carried out by **MacMillan Bloedel**, a member of the **Canadian Pulp and Paper Association**, highlights the importance of assessing the effects of habitat protection measures on wildlife habitat and the economics of timber extraction. The study shows that, as might be expected, although zoning – allowing timber harvesting to proceed in a restricted area – would reduce the volume of timber logged, it would produce more wildlife habitat than if logging were to be carried out across the landscape. The latter practice was also found to introduce higher infrastructure costs, increased habitat fragmentation and reduced long-term return when compared with zoning. The results demonstrate that habitat protection and economics are not necessarily opposing factors in such operations.

Chemicals company **ICI** has developed an international nature conservation monitoring program. Known as Nature Link, the program is probably one of the largest initiatives of its kind. It has recorded more than 1,000 species of birds and 150 species of mammals on its sites across the world, some of them recognized as being internationally endangered. The company is a major land owner whose properties include habitats ranging from woodland and heathland to mangrove swamps and rain forests. Nature Link conservation programs are run by ICI employees in partnership with local and international conservation groups, ensuring proper habitat and species management. The information generated by Nature Link is being loaded onto a computer database, which will soon be made available to interested parties.

The need for policies and strategies

Inventories of biodiversity are needed, too, for the development of national strategies or policies – blueprints for the conservation and sustainable use of a nation's biological resources. Many countries already have national environment and/or development strategies in place and these can serve as a useful starting point for the more detailed biodiversity strategies which each Contracting Party to the Convention is required to develop. The process for preparing the blueprints is usually an open and consultative one, so there are many opportunities for business to become involved.

However, many large enterprises have already gone a step beyond this by developing their own strategies for conserving biodiversity. **Ontario Hydro**, North America's largest electric utility, has found that its biodiversity strategy has not only helped it plan and monitor its own actions, but that it has also helped enhance the company's image in the eyes of conservation groups. One of the ways in which the company is helping conserve biodiversity is through a series of investigations, including one into the effects on biodiversity of woodland fragmentation by high voltage transmission lines. Ecological models derived from field studies have been used to identify and protect woodlands of particular importance to songbirds and migrating species. Techniques developed in this study have been widely used by provincial agencies for the selection of other woodland sites in North America.

Environmental standards are also a major concern for **DuPont** which, in the case of its production plants in Asturias, northern Spain, even went so far as to make protection of the environment a condition of employment. A long-term biodiversity plan was developed at the site-permitting stage in conjunction with local government, environmental non-governmental organizations (NGOs) and the University of Oviedo. Among the many activities set in motion were the restoration of a large wetland site, planting of 140,000 trees, and support of an environmental education program in the local community. The targets established for the company's plant included zero emissions by progressively eliminating waste and preventing releases, including air emissions, solid and liquid wastes and aqueous discharge. Groundwater protection was also included, a feature which has since been adopted as a model at all the company's sites. Environmental monitoring programs have been put in place to ensure that mitigation measures are adequate and effectively implemented.

The importance of strategies such as these is now becoming well recognized by many companies. For example, the Danish pharmaceutical and biotechnological company, Novo Nordisk, as part of its defined position on biodiversity, has declared that it:

- acknowledges the Convention's emphasis on the sovereign rights of states to their own natural resources and, furthermore, recognizes that benefits arising from the use of biological resources should be subject to a fair and equitable system of sharing

- intends to collaborate with research organizations with high standards of expertise from many different regions of the world, that collaboration being compensated by financial agreements, the training of scientists, or transfer of technology

- encourages governments to authorize leading institutes and universities to enter into international cooperation within the field of research and development on the sustainable use of resources. Prior to signing a contract, cooperating organizations are required to obtain clearance with relevant domestic authorities with regard to the Convention on Biological Diversity. Where materials are derived from a third-party country, Novo Nordisk requires that its suppliers ensure that compensation is given to the country of origin, as specified in a previously arranged contract.

Benefiting local communities

The Convention on Biological Diversity has recognized the need to include local communities in actions related to conservation and sustainable use. Already there are many examples where local communities benefit from projects supported by the private sector. In Mexico, for example, UNAM, Mexico's Autonomous National University, has received financial support from CEMEX for research on, and the management of, protected areas, as well as for specific projects to monitor the population levels of threatened wild fauna. The project is managed by environmental non-governmental organizations (NGOs), local communities, universities and private groups, and is yet another instance of local industry supporting biodiversity management in a way that not only benefits local wildlife but also yields new job opportunities.

Business can also take a more direct approach to supporting communities through training. For example, it can help selected groups to become better at managing natural resources, or it can finance habitat restoration projects. The latter is one of the activities being undertaken by the **Thai Farmers Bank**, which is working with the government of Thailand, local communities, monasteries and members of the private sector on a reforestation project in Chiangmai Province. The main environmental issues being tackled include flood control and the prevention of drought, atmospheric pollution and local poverty.

Habitat protection and enhancement for sustainable development has also been at the forefront of an award-winning project implemented by **General Motors** of Canada, with support from local government and communities. Following a master plan developed in 1986, a former dairy farm situated on the shoreline of the McLaughlin Bay Wildlife Reserve has been actively managed to protect and promote local biodiversity. Stewardship of this important site has included the development of recreation and public-awareness facilities. To allow handicapped people to learn more about nature, multi-sensory trails and other special amenities have been constructed so they can appreciate their surroundings by using their sense of touch, smell and hearing. Monitoring of wildlife populations is also a continuing part of the management program.

Biodiversity and indigenous knowledge

Many business sectors have already realized the benefits of applying indigenous knowledge. In the agricultural sector, for example, a blend of new and traditional knowledge, technologies and strategies has been used to improve agro-systems in many parts of the world. Small-scale potato farmers in Nepal, Kenya and Peru independently developed a diffused-light technique that reduced the sprouting of stored potatoes. The **International Potato Center** in Peru has been disseminating this cost-effective and environmentally healthy technique through its international extension projects to potato farmers in many other countries.

Developing partnerships for the future

A united approach is essential for conserving biodiversity. As the preceding examples have shown, partnerships tackling a wide range of biodiversity topics have already been established between the private sector and other branches of society. But many other cases might be cited.

In Pennsylvania, USA, for example, a joint fact-finding project is under way between the **National Audubon Society** and **The Procter & Gamble Company** to develop recommendations for managing wildlife habitat in private forests. The aim is to understand the links between timber harvesting systems and the resultant wildlife habitat value. At present, many of the private forests in that region are harvested without advice or guidance from professional foresters. Training and education programs for loggers and land-owners are seen as key tools for promoting sustainable and responsible forestry in private, non-industrial hardwood forests, and this project has been developed to close this knowledge gap. Scientists, local stakeholders (including independent loggers and private non-industrial land-owners) as well as local and regional conservation experts and government agencies have been involved in the process. This demonstrates the promise and results which can be expected by successful partnerships working towards a common goal.

Another effective partnership has been developed between **BHP Petroleum** and **The Nature Conservancy** in Pecos County, Texas, USA. Situated in the western part of the state, the unusual ecological conditions of the Diamond Y Spring Preserve have long attracted attention. Several rare and endangered species of fauna and flora have been recorded from the saline springs that flow through the Preserve, a feature which led to The Nature Conservancy purchasing the site in 1990. Although oil and gas extraction had been carried out since the 1970s, BHP Petroleum's policy of minimal interference and impact, imposed from the outset, greatly contributed to the welfare of the site. A series of mutually beneficial discussions between the two organizations led to concrete actions which have helped restore and manage the site. They ranged from habitat restoration in abandoned drilling locations and other sites, to the general improvement of the region's aesthetic beauty, and the introduction of nature tours for interested groups.

In China, **Johnson & Johnson** is working with the **World Wide Fund for Nature (WWF)** in support of the Trade Records Analysis of Flora and Fauna in Commerce (TRAFFIC) which is undertaking a comprehensive assessment of the trade in rhino and tiger parts for use in traditional medicines. Information that will influence the policy of the Chinese government and CITES (the Convention on International Trade in Endangered Species of Wild Fauna and Flora) has already been obtained as a result of this initiative and has provided a better understanding of the status of traditional medicine in China. Partly as a result of TRAFFIC's efforts, China has made some progress in reducing the illicit trade and in training conservation officers to detect illegal products. It has also started a state-sanctioned research and development effort to identify medicinal substitutes for products that now use endangered species.

One final example of successful collaboration: **Unilever** and **WWF** have recently formed a conservation partnership to create market incentives for sustainable fishing. In a clear signal that common ground has been established between these organizations, a Marine Stewardship Council has been established as an independent, non-profit making, non-governmental body with a broad set of principles for sustainable fishing. Only fisheries meeting set standards will be eligible for certification by independent, accrediting firms.

The foregoing initiatives all demonstrate how effective business can be when it works in partnership with other interested parties. They show that the private sector is already contributing to the conservation and sustainable use of biodiversity through a broad and varied range of actions. Its involvement is now increasingly being recognized by other sectors of society, so providing a solid foundation for even greater opportunities for collaboration and for a strengthened approach towards the common goal of conserving biodiversity for everyone.

7. Engaging the private sector in the Convention

Business can participate in the biodiversity debate at three levels international, national and company. Here we suggest practical steps companies can take to get involved at each level and we outline an action plan for management.

How can business participate?

In the earlier sections of this guide we explained how and why biodiversity is important for business. Section 6 presented case examples to show the positive steps already taken by a number of companies to deal with conservation and sustainable use issues. However, many companies are working in isolation or, at best, in cooperation with a small number of local organizations and communities.

While action at the local level is a prerequisite for successful long-term conservation, business activities could be greatly strengthened and made more influential if they were set within a framework of coordinated national and international actions, such as the one provided by the Convention on Biological Diversity. So, to repeat the basic message of this guide, it is vital that business begins to participate in this framework so that its interests are represented and so that its expertise is included in the development of government policies and programs, and in guidelines and other management tools.

The aim of this section is to offer some practical suggestions about how business can involve itself. There are three key entry levels:

✓ **International** – international meetings and deliberations on biodiversity programs
✓ **National** – national obligations set out by the Convention and decisions taken by the Conference of the Parties (COP)
✓ **Company** – developing in-house biodiversity policies and strategies to manage the biological resources the company affects and also the concerns of local communities and other stakeholders

We shall look at each in turn.

Business participation at the international level

Business can contribute to the development of the Convention by participating at the COP and SBSTTA meetings, and the meetings of the Global Biodiversity Forum (GBF)[1] and other inter-sessional meetings (see the Calendar below). There is also much scope for direct discussions with governments.

1997	**August 29-31, Montreal**	Calendar
	Global Biodiversity Forum (GBF)	
	To discuss topics of concern to the implementation process of the Convention on Biological Diversity	Significant events for business involvement in the Convention
	September 1-5, Montreal	
	SBSTTA 3	
	Discussions to include fresh waters and biodiversity impact assessment	
	October 13-17, Montreal	
	Ad hoc Expert Group on Biosafety	
	October 13-22, Turkey	
	Forestry for Sustainable Development	
1998	**May 1-3, Bratislava**	
	Global Biodiversity Forum session for COP 4	
	May 4-15, COP 4, Bratislava	

Please note that the dates and/or venues of some of these meetings are likely to change. Updates of these as well as details of other relevant meetings may be obtained on the Internet from the Web pages of many of the organizations listed at the back of this guide, or by contacting the Secretariat of the Convention on Biological Diversity.

---

[1] The Global Biodiversity Forum is a stakeholder's meeting organized by UNEP, IUCN, the World Resources Institute and other organizations. It is usually held before COP and/or SBSTTA meetings to provide a forum for discussion by all stakeholders of the main agenda points of the later meetings.

In addition, new policies and protocols are currently being discussed. Examples are those on Biosafety, Indigenous Peoples, and Intellectual Property Rights. Each of these areas needs to be monitored by business and to receive input from it. Companies should therefore ensure that their interests are represented at important meetings either via cross sectoral business groups such as the WBCSD, sectoral associations or directly by individual companies.

We described in Section 5 the main programs that will be developed by the Conference of the Parties for COP 4 and which directly affect business. They are summarized here in Box 9.

<table>
<tr><td>

Box 9

Emerging programs
on biodiversity by
the COP

</td><td>

Financial resources
- new and additional investments in biodiversity, including private sector investments

Incentive measures
- design and implementation of incentive measures

Biodiversity impact assessment

Marine ecosystems
- development and implementation of integrated coastal zone management programs

Agriculture issues
- genetic resources – use of resources; benefit sharing; and safety issues
- over-dependence on agrochemicals

Freshwater ecosystems
- ecosystem focus

Terrestrial ecosystems
- conservation, sustainable use, and benefit sharing
- development of biodiversity policies for mining, forestry, fishing and other sectors
- integration of the Convention's objectives into sustainable forestry management
- *in-situ* conservation
- habitat restoration initiatives and monitoring

Genetic resources
- development of national guidelines

Intellectual property rights
- review of Convention issues with WTO and TRIPS

Clearing-House Mechanism
- technical expertise for the development of internet link for all COP members

</td></tr>
</table>

Business participation at the national level

A key entry point here is through the individual country's national bio-diversity planning process. While some countries have established such a strategy, many others are currently in the process of doing so. The knowledge and expertise of the private sector is badly needed in these processes.

In addition, individual companies need to develop their own strategies and policies to reflect or recognize the national biodiversity strategy. Companies which fail to do so may find themselves unaware of the main issues and isolated from the formulation of current government policy. They should therefore contact the government institution responsible for biodiversity and planning in order to establish a dialogue and to discuss developments and possible ways of collaborating under the framework of the national strategy.

As well as becoming familiar with and involved in the overall national biodiversity strategy, business should keep abreast of discussions and developments on national guidelines for incentive measures, biosafety, intellectual property rights, monitoring of biodiversity indicators, and other topics now being debated within the Convention process. These issues need to be addressed at the national level in the first instance and they require specific company input before being presented by the Parties to the COP.

Business participation at the company level

We have seen that many aspects of the Convention can have a bearing, either directly or indirectly, on the operations of individual companies. And notwithstanding the crucial need for business to participate in the framework-setting process that takes place at the national and interna-tional level, for many companies it is at the local level that the effects of the Convention will be most keenly felt and where the opportunities for action are at the greatest.

To help companies to become more involved with these issues and to ini-tiate the first stages of formulating a biodiversity management plan, we present below a brief guide to the main steps they will need to take. The outline is not intended to be a comprehensive environmental management plan for biodiversity, but it should serve to highlight the main issues that need to be taken into consideration in order to conserve and manage biodiversity in the area in which the company operates.

Developing a management plan

We believe that a properly devised plan for managing biodiversity within a company will include most, if not all, of the following eight elements:

1. The company should develop a formal **biodiversity policy**, or should incorporate biodiversity into its existing environmental policy. This sends an important signal to employees and to outside observers that the company takes seriously its responsibility for managing biodiversity sustainably.

2. The company should identify and **comply with national policies** and laws on biodiversity conservation.

3. It should develop a **biodiversity strategy** which aims to conserve species and ecosystem biodiversity through conservation and the sustainable use of the biological resources the company manages or affects. The strategy should:

    ✓ focus on those operations which affect biological resources, in order to ensure that there is no threat to, or loss of, native species, populations and ecosystems
    ✓ be developed with the national biodiversity strategy as a guideline and be compiled in cooperation with all the company's different business units
    ✓ adopt an ecosystem approach to the management of biodiversity, such an approach to include the development of methodologies for ecosystem-based environmental impact assessments (EIAs)
    ✓ be integrated at all stages in the life-cycle of the company's products, processes or services, including their planning and operation

4. The company should work actively with other organizations, such as government institutions and wildlife/conservation organizations, as well as the general public, **sharing information and knowledge** with them about the management of significant species and ecosystems.

5. Company management should ensure that **local communities** are closely involved with decisions affecting the use of natural resources. One way to do this is to invite local community representatives to monitor the progress of relevant projects such as *in-situ* research on sustainable forest management or rehabilitation programs. Local communities can include a variety of stakeholders.

Of particular importance in some areas is the indigenous peoples' knowledge and the specific issues related to their use of, and relationship to, the land and biological resources. This relationship needs to be harnessed in a positive way, both for the company and the peoples, by developing agreements which promote the equitable sharing of resources.

Local projects should also integrate cross-sectoral expertise by including academic groups and non-governmental organizations (NGOs) in resource-management projects. This ensures that all stakeholders are involved to some degree in the decision-making process. In a number of countries where biodiversity features strongly in the local Agenda 21 process, there are opportunities for participation and leadership by the business sector.

6. Conservation of biodiversity should be at the heart of the company's biodiversity strategy. This means it should try to retain natural areas where possible, to restore degraded areas, and to harvest resources sustainably. Understanding the importance of *in-situ* **conservation** can help focus a company's attention on developing management plans which integrate conservation with sustainable development. This might, for example, entail defining conservation areas within existing company land, developing buffer zones around its operations, or promoting the **sustainable use** of resources such as timber and non-timber products in forestry operations.

7. Active **partnerships** to assist and promote the conservation of biodiversity should be a vital component of the company's biodiversity strategy.

8. Regular and **continuing education** of employees, suppliers, stakeholders and local communities is important, both to increase public awareness and to ensure that biodiversity conservation is considered in all the company's activities.

The next step

Our aim in producing this guide has been to help business unravel some of the complexities of the Convention on Biological Diversity and to show companies how to identify openings through which they can become involved in the continuing dialogue on the development of the Convention.

If a company can integrate the key objectives of the Convention into its daily operations, it is likely to receive greater recognition of its programs from the broader constituency. This approach will give the company a far stronger position with conservation organizations and other interested parties, and that position will be achieved in a manner which should be mutually rewarding and produce ecologically beneficial outcomes.

For this to work, however, it is essential that there is a feedback process in the mechanisms suggested in this report. Actions taken at the company level must in some way link back to those being taken at the national level and, in turn, to those at the international level too. A two-way flow of information and ideas is therefore vital. In the absence of such a link, business risks being marginalized and having to work alone outside the Convention.

Both the WBCSD and IUCN are willing and eager to help companies play a more active and visible role in this process and want to help forge a lasting and mutually beneficial relationship between business and the other parties involved in the Convention on Biological Diversity. This guide is the first stage of this process.

We are hopeful that business will recognize what is at stake and will respond to the challenge.

Speaking a common language

Conservation, as with any business, has developed its own language. The following are among the most common scientific terms used when discussing biodiversity, the Convention and related topics.

Access to genetic resources
The facilitation of equitable access to genetic resources and their subsequent use.

Benefit sharing
The fair and equitable sharing of the benefits arising from the use of biological resources, especially genetic resources.

Biological diversity
The variability among living organisms from all sources including, inter alia, terrestrial, marine and other aquatic ecosystems and the ecological complexes of which they are part; this includes diversity within species, between species and of ecosystems.

Biological resources
Genetic resources, organisms or parts thereof, populations, or any other biotic component of ecosystems with actual or potential use or value for humanity.

Bioprospecting
Exploration of biodiversity for commercially valuable genetic and biochemical resources.

Biosafety
Defined in the Convention as "the safe transfer, handling and use of any living modified organism resulting from biotechnology".

Biotechnology
A technique which uses living organisms to make or modify a product, to improve plants and animals, or to develop microorganisms for specific purposes.

Clearing-House Mechanism

A facility established by the Conference of the Parties to ensure that information and experiences are shared among interested parties.

Country of origin
(of genetic resources)

The country which possesses those genetic resources in *in-situ* conditions.

Ecosystem

A term used to describe how organisms interact with one another and their environment.

Ex-situ conservation

A form of "off-site" conservation intended to keep selected organisms (seed, pollen, semen or individual organisms) alive outside their original habitat or natural environment for the purposes of captive breeding, propagation and potential later re-introduction.

Genebank

Facility established for the *ex-situ* conservation of seeds, tissues or reproductive cells of animals or plants.

Genetic engineering

Modification of the genetic structure of living organisms using molecular biology techniques that can transfer genes between dissimilar organisms.

Genetic resources

Genetic materials of actual or potential value.

Global Environment Facility (GEF)

An international fund managed by the World Bank, UNDP and UNEP. It funds projects in developing countries which are directed towards global protection of the environment.

Habitat

The place or type of site where an organism or population occurs naturally.

In-situ conservation

In-situ conservation aims to preserve ecosystems so that processes, habitats and species can continue to evolve in a natural manner. Protected areas have been one of the main ways of ensuring *in-situ* conservation: however, this is seen as inadequate as many ecosystems are not adequately represented.

Intellectual property rights

To promote and protect innovation by allowing the "owner" of the knowledge to have security over his/her invention for a designated period of time.

National strategy

Each country will develop a national strategy to implement the obligations of the Convention.

Species

A population whose members are able to interbreed freely under natural conditions.

Sustainable use

The use of components of biological diversity in a way and at a rate that does not lead to the long-term decline of biological diversity, thereby maintaining its potential to meet the needs and aspirations of present and future generations.

Contacting the biodiversity community

The following is a selection of some of the main international organizations working on the implementation of the Convention on Biological Diversity. Please note that some of the details given below are likely to change.

Biodiversity Conservation Information Systems (BCIS)
Rue Mauverney 28
CH-1196 Gland
Switzerland
Tel: +41 22 999 0001
Fax: +41 22 999 0002
URL:http:// biodiversity.org

Global Environment Facility (GEF)
1818 H Street
NW, Washington D.C. 20433
U.S.A.
Tel: +1 202 473 8324
Fax: + 1 202 522 3240
URL:http://www.worldbank.org/html/gef

IUCN — The World Conservation Union
Rue Mauverney 28
CH-1196 Gland
Switzerland
Tel: +41 22 999 0001
Fax: +41 22 999 0002
URL: http://iucn.org

United Nations Environment Program (UNEP)
P.O. Box 30552
Nairobi
Kenya
Tel: +254 2 62 1234
Fax: +254 2 62 3927
URL: http://www.unep.org

World Business Council for Sustainable Development
160 Route de Florissant
CH-1231 Conches-Geneva
Switzerland
Tel: +41 22 839 3100
Fax: +41 22 839 3131
URL: http://www.wbcsd.ch

World Resources Institute
1790 New York Avenue, NW
Washington, D.C. 20006
U.S.A.
Tel: +1 202 638 6300
Fax: +1 202 638 0036
URL: http://www.wri.org

World Wide Fund For Nature (WWF)
Avenue du Mont-Blanc
CH-1196 Gland
Switzerland
Tel: +41 22 364 9111
Fax: +41 22 364 5358
URL: http://www.panda.org

For more information

Published references

Baumann, M., Bell, J., Koechlin, F. and Pimbert, M. 1996. *The Life Industry. Biodiversity, People and Profits.* Intermediate Technology Publications, London.

Biodiversity Bulletin. A tool for promoting effective implementation of the Convention on Biological Diversity. Produced by the Biodiversity Action Network, Washington, D.C.

Di Castri, F. and Younès, T. 1996. *Biodiversity, Science and Development.* CAB International.

Glowka, L., Burhenne-Guilmin, F. and Synge, H. 1994. *A Guide to the Convention on Biological Diversity.* IUCN, Gland, Switzerland.

Potter, C.S., Cohen, J.I. and Janczewski, D. 1993. *Perspectives of Biodiversity: Case studies of genetic resource conservation and development.* AAAS Publications, Washington, D.C.

Reid, W., Laird, S., Meyer, C.A., Gámez, R., Sittenfeld, A., Janzen, D.H., Gollin, M.A. and Juma, C. 1993. *Biodiversity Prospecting: Using Genetic Resources for Sustainable Development.* World Resources Institute, Washington, D.C.

WWF. 1996. *WWF Guide to Forest Certification.* WWF International, Gland, Switzerland.

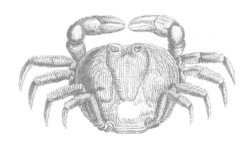

Information contributed to this guide

IUCN and the WBCSD would like to thank all of these companies and organizations for their willingness to provide information to this guide. Except when indicated by an asterisk, all the companies are members of the WBCSD.

Aracruz Celulose SA
Avenor Inc.
Business Council for Sustainable Development for the Gulf of Mexico
Business Council for Sustainable Development for Indonesia
         Majelis Usahawan Indonesia *
Business Council for Sustainable Development for Latin America
         CEMEX *
         Companhia Vale do Rio Doce
         S.P.R. Fuente Clara del Sureste *
BHP Petroleum
Bowater Mersey Paper Company Ltd *
Canadian Pulp and Paper Association *
         MacMillan Bloedel Ltd. *
Ducks Unlimited de Mexico, A.C. *
Dutch Electricity Generating Board *
DuPont
Face Foundation *
General Motors Corporation
Glaxo Wellcome Plc
ICI
International Paper Company
Johnson & Johnson
Merck and Company Inc. *
NEC Corporation
Noranda Inc.
Novartis International AG
Novo Nordisk A/S
Ontario Hydro
Rio Tinto
Samsung Electronics
Stora
Thai Farmers Bank Public Company Limited
TransAlta Corporation
The Dow Chemical Company
The Procter & Gamble Company
The Tokyo Electric Power Co.
Unilever N.V.
Westvaco Corporation
WMC Limited

1399 147